Michèle-Caroline Heck

THE GOLDEN BOOK OF
ALSACE

STRASBOURG • COLMAR • MULHOUSE • WISSEMBOURG
NIEDERBRONN-LES-BAINS • HAGUENAU • SAVERNE
HAUT-BARR • MOLSHEIM • ROSHEIM • SELESTAT
BARR • MONT SAINTE-ODILE • OBERNAI • KINTZHEIM
HAUT-KŒNIGSBOURG • RIBEAUVILLE • EGUISHEIM
RIQUEWIHR • KAYSERSBERG • TURCKHEIM
GUEBWILLER • ROUFFACH • MUNSTER
MURBACH • THANN • HUNAWIHR

BONECHI

CONTENTS

Distributeur en Alsace

EDITION PFISTER
2 Rue Alfred Kastler - 67300 SCHILTIGHEIM - TEL. 88 83 93 94 - FAX 88 33 29 00

Photographs from the archives of the Publishing House excepting those taken by *Jean Pierre Théophile*: pages 8, 10 right, 49, 56,
63 top, 66 right, 68, 76, 90, 91 top, 93, 96 centre and bottom. *A. Stern*: pages 9, 37, 48. *A.M. Breger*: pages 10 left, 43, 66 left.
Kronenberger: page 16. *Yves Noto Campanella*: page 50.
Pages 32 bottom and 33 bottom: photos kindly supplied by the *Municipality of Strasbourg*. Page 92 top: photo kindly supplied by the
Musée Français du Chemin-de-Fer, Mulhouse. Page 92 centre and bottom: photo kindly supplied by the
Musée National de l'Automobile, Mulhouse.
Pages 94-95: photos kindly supplied by the *Ecomusée d'Alsace, Mulhouse*. Page 96 top: photo kindly supplied by the
Jardin des Papillons Exotiques Vivants, Hunawihr.

ISBN 88-8029-140-8

INTRODUCTION

The great variety of natural scenery in Alsace is dominated by the presence of the plain which links the green hilly country of Sundgau in the south to the Wissembourg region and the Outre-Forêt in the north. To the east the game-filled region of Ried lies between it and the Rhine. To the west the foothills of the Vosges extend their vine-covered slopes for nearly 100 kilometres. Finally dominating the whole in the south and gradually trailing off towards the north are the Vosges themselves, that ancient mountain mass whose well worn peaks culminate in the Grand Ballon at an altitude of 1424 metres.

The first traces of civilisation in Alsace, the remains of dwellings and burial places, date back to the Neolithic Period. Round about 1500 B.C. the Protocelts first colonized the Hagenau region and then little by little occupied the whole of Alsace. Alsace, the principal gateway into France at the time of the great invasions, underwent a radical transformation both as regards its economy and its way of life, at the end of the Bronze Age. Its agriculture became fixed, fortresses were built in the Vosges and villages developed in the plain. The mainly agricultural population was opened up to outside influences especially those from Italy. During the 3rd and 2nd centuries B.C. Alsace was partially resettled by Gaulish tribes from the west and the south. Thus the Sequanes in the south and the Mediomatrics in the north were replaced by the Tribocs.

After Julius Caesar's victory over Ariovistus in 58 B.C. Alsace entered the Roman sphere of influence and the Rhine became a frontier guarded by a series of "castella" – Kembs, Brisach, Strasbourg, Seltz. The present borders of Alsace do not correspond entirely with those of the Roman period. Divided into a number of territories it was criss-crossed by a dense network of roads and the most important places were Strasbourg ("Argentorate"), Saverne ("Tres Tabernae"), Brumath (the capital of Lower Alsace), Horbourg ("Argentovaria"), and Seltz ("Saletio"). This civilisation was essentially agricultural, artisanal (smithies, pottery and glass-making workshops) and commercial.

After a period of relative calm, invasions and civil wars followed each other until 451 A.D. when Attila and the Huns swept down on Alsace and destroyed the last vestiges of the Gallo-Roman civilisation. The integration of Alsace into the kingdom of the Franks after the victory of Clovis over the Alamans in 496 A.D. remains very obscure.

In the 7th century the Duchy of Alsace appears for the first time as a political and administrative unit. Its most famous duke was undoubtedly Etichon, the father of St. Odile. This period saw the foundation of numerous abbeys, due mainly to the efforts of St. Firmin who introduced the Benedictine Order, in particular at Marmoutier and Murbach, and of the Bishop of Strasbourg who was also the head of the civil administration. It was in this period too that the name Alsace ("Alesacius") appeared for the first time.

In the 9th century the Duchy was divided into two Counties: Nordgau and Sundgau corresponding to the bishoprics of Strasbourg and Basle. The reign of Charlemagne was a period of peace and prosperity, but afterwards Alsace was caught up in the quarrels over the succession of Louis the Pious, Charlemagne's son, who was betrayed and then captured by his sons at the Champ du Mensonge (the Field of Deceit) near Colmar. In 842 by the Oath of Strasbourg, drawn up in the Romanic and Tudesque languages, Charles the Bald and Louis of Bavaria swore to come to each other's aid and assistance against their brother Lotho I. In 843 after the division of Verdun, Charles the Bald became king of France, Louis king of Bavaria and Lotho retained Lotharingia, a region which included Alsace and stretched far beyond the Rhine corridor extending from Frisia to Lombardy. In 961 Otho founded the Holy Roman Empire of which Alsace remained a part until the 17th century, becoming a "territory of the empire". Otho based his power on the church, virtually making the bishops princes at the service of his policies.

From the 11th to the 13th centuries Alsace underwent expansion in all areas. A renaissance of the towns was favoured by the development of trade, land was cleared and cultivated, new religious foundations appeared, especially those of the Mendicant orders, and the arts and letters flourished in the towns, the castles and the monasteries. However the 11th century was much troubled by the "Quarrel over the Investitures" which involved a confrontation between the bishops and the aristocracy led by the Hohenstaufen family. Moreover by the middle of the 12th century the authority of the latter in Alsace was paramount. They were great builders and from their stronghold, the Pfalz of Hagenau, they organised the construction of numerous churches and castles in the Vosges which they entrusted to loyal vassels. Frederick II, the foremost figure among them, was the founder of numerous walled towns. In this he was imitated by other lords such as the seigneur de Ferrette.

His death in 1250 marked the end of the dynasty. This collapse signaled the start of a long struggle between the bishops and the towns under the protection of Rudolph of Hapsburg, the Count or Landgrave of Upper Alsace who was elected king and who founded the Hapsburg dynasty. He endowed the towns with more liberal statutes, raising some of them to the status of "towns of the Empire", and as a consequence they became the source of his power.

A period of decline, starting in the 14th century, was marked by epidemics, political instability and the struggle between Louis IV of Bavaria and Philip the Handsome. In order to combat this atmosphere of instability the Alsatian towns joined together in an alliance with both defensive and offensive aims. The towns of the Decapole were Colmar, Mulhouse, Munster, Turckheim, Kaysersberg, Sélestat, Obernai, Rosheim, Wissembourg and Hagenau. The towns grew, the arts and crafts and commerce developed and the burgers and corporations took an ever greater part in the running of urban government.

The 15th century was marked by intense artistic and

cultural activity and an apparent prosperity which, however, covered up a host of problems and latent conflicts. Strasbourg became Lutheran and Mulhouse became Calvinist. The peasant uprising which took its impetus from religious differences became widespread. The Guerre des Rustauds (the Rustics' War) saw the peasants in open opposition to the nobility and especially to the Bishop of Strasbourg. However the uprising was rapidly repressed.

During the 16th and 17th centuries Alsace was a country divided into numerous small domains, but these gradually joined together in federations which eventually gave rise to the Etats Généraux, the local parliament of Alsace. The Counter-Reformation, led by the Jesuits from their base in Molsheim, attempted to overturn the Protestantism so firmly implanted in Strasbourg. During the 17th century the economic activity due to Alsace's position as a commercial cross-roads, which assured the supremacy of the bourgeoisie, slowly declined. It was particularly affected by the Thirty Years War. In 1632 Swedish troops occupied the Alsatian strongholds and in 1634 the French army occupied the whole of Alsace. In 1635 Colmar was placed under the protection of the French Crown and the Treaties of Westphalia handed over Hapsburg possessions in Alsace to the king of France. However at that time the whole of Alsace was not yet joined to the French Crown. The towns of the Decapole, the episcopal lands and Strasbourg itself were the last parts of Alsace to be annexed on the 30th September 1681.

Thus did French culture penetrate Alsace.

In 1790 the two départements of Bas-Rhin and Haut-Rhin were created and the frontier was moved from the Vosges to the Rhine. Alsace, apart from Mulhouse which had to wait until 1798, was entirely integrated into France with whose destiny it was now linked.

The 19th century was mainly marked by the tremendous industrial development, especially of the textile industry in Mulhouse and the valley of the Vosges, and by the development of communications such as the opening of the Basle-Strasbourg-Paris railway lines.

In 1870, in spite of continuing protests by the Alsatians, Alsace was annexed to the 2nd Reich of the Hohenzollerns. It was not until after the First World War that Alsace was returned to France under the terms of the treaty of Versailles. Although very badly affected by the Second World War Alsace rose again from the ruins. In 1949 Strasbourg became the European capital and a remarkable industrial, commercial and agricultural expansion contributed to its development.

However in spite of this international dimension Alsace remains a region which is very much alive and attached to its own traditions, to its dialect which is still widely spoken, and to its cuisine. Apart from the great popular celebrations such as the harvest and wine making festivals, many other customs, often linked to religious traditions, such as the Easter Hare who is the bearer of brightly coloured eggs or St. Nicholas, are still celebrated.

The crucifixes, calvaries and small chapels which can

be seen at cross-roads, the entry to villages or on the passes of the Vosges are a constant reminder of popular piety. The oldest date from the 15th century but the majority are later being of 17th, 18th or even 19th century date. Even if the costumes and other aspects of folklore which are seen in the Wine Festivals of a number of villages show a loss of traditional richness and variety, the architecture of many of these villages still bears witness to the vitality of the ancient tradition of vine and wine. In the following pages we are able to show only a few examples of this architectural richness.

Wine is not the only important tradition in this region of France, there is another one which is found in every part of Alsace, the stork. For most people it is the very symbol of Alsace. The ancient affection of the region for these long-legged birds is not in any doubt and as long ago as the 13th century the chronicles recorded their dates of arrival from North Africa where they spend the winter. The decrease in the number of these birds, at first quite slow, has been marked in Alsace since 1950. It would be wrong to attribute the cause of this decrease entirely to the disappearance of the Ried marshes and of their frogs. The various attempts to raise the birds artificially and to reintroduce breeding pairs will only stand a chance of succeeding if they are accompanied by a widespread attempt to safeguard the natural environment which is still one of Alsace's major resources.

A stork's nest.

A typical crucifix
in a vineyard.

WISSEMBOURG

Situated in the extreme north of Alsace, Wissembourg, surrounded by its city wall planted with lime trees, is a typical example of a small Alsatian town. Its position between the two winding arms of the river Lauter gives the town a particular charm with the half-timbered houses lining both sides of the Lauter in places, for example, on the Quai du Marais or in the Bruch area. The 1448 Salt House with its many-tiered monumental roof has retained its original appearance.

A good example of 18th century architecture is the Town Hall (built by Massol in 1749) with its belfry in the middle of the façade. This is a reminder of one of the great moments of Wissembourg's history when the exiled Polish king Stanislas Lezczynski and his daughter Marie were living there.

The town is dominated by two pieces of religious architecture. The church of St. Peter and St. Paul was founded at the end of the 8th century but the oldest surviving parts, the west tower and a part of the chapel in the cloisters, only date from the end of the 11th century. In the 13th century reconstruction started at the eastern end of the church, the choir and the north side of the transept being consecrated in 1284, while the nave was only finished in the 14th century. This church with its beautiful stained glass is outstanding in the region in spite of the lack of unity in its construction, emphasised by damage and by changes in later periods. It is the largest church in Alsace after Strasbourg cathedral. The church of St. John-the-Baptist, much smaller and built in the Gothic style, is right next to the city wall.

This short survey of Wissembourg would be incomplete without a mention of all those religious buildings, churches and convents, which have been demolished in the course of the centuries and which serve to remind us of the past grandeur of this town.

Wissembourg: aerial view of the town.

NIEDERBRONN-
LES-BAINS

Niederbronn's development as a tourist centre and as the most important spa in Alsace, is due to its situation and its two springs. Already in Roman times baths had been built close to the two springs. These two springs, one of which gushes forth in the centre of the town opposite the Casino and was known to the Celts, while the other emerges near the north exit of the town, are both endowed with various curative properties.

The baths were restored for the first time in the 16th century by Count Philippe de Hanau. During the Second Empire this spa enjoyed enormous prosperity. Badly damaged during the last war, Niederbronn has recovered from the destruction by developing other aspects of tourism in addition to that of a spa town. Summer tourism is based partly on the existence of the Casino and its gaming tables, but above all on the beauty of the site which makes it the natural starting point for large numbers of excursions into the northern Vosges, so liberally endowed with ruined castles or "Burg". Examples are Wasenbourg, a 14th century castle built next to a Roman temple, which greatly impressed Goethe; Falkenstein, the falcon's rock; and the Keep of the 14th century Waldeck castle which overlooks the picturesque Hanau mere.

◀ *Wissembourg: the Town Hall.*

◀ *Wissembourg: the Salt House.*

Haguenau: Tour des Chevaliers or
the Knights' Tower.

Haguenau: the Museum and the Historic Library.

Haguenau: St. George's church. ▶

HAGUENAU

Situated in the middle of an immense forest covering 20,000 hectares, Haguenau has today lost the dominant role which it had in the Middle Ages.

The forest of Haguenau, known as the "Sacred Forest" both because of the numerous tumuli, many of which have never been explored, and because of the large numbers of monasteries and hermitages built there, was undoubtedly the major reason for the great predilection which the emperors had for this town. Frederick Barbarossa had an Imperial castle built here — a Pfalz — in whose chapel were kept the "Crown Jewels of the Holy Roman Empire", the crown, the sceptre, the globe and the sword. His successors, Henry VI, Frederick of Hohenstaufen and Rudolph of Hapsburg also made it their preferred residence.

The remains of the medieval city, which during the 14th century housed the executive council of the Decapole, are few and far between. Not many of the 54 towers and 29 churches remain. Examples are the Tour des Pêcheurs or Fishermen's Tower, the Tour des Chevaliers or Knights' Tower and the churches of St. George and St. Nicholas. The whole town was sacked by the troops of the Marshal of Créqui in 1677 and the castle was entirely destroyed.

St. George's church has undergone many changes since its foundation. Of the original church only the two towers either side of the Gothic apse now remain. The Romanesque nave which was finished in 1189 originally had a wooden ceiling. The 13th century reconstruction of the choir and the transept incorporated earlier parts. The church still has very beautiful furniture, sculpture, paintings and liturgical objects dating from the 15th and 16th centuries.

SAVERNE

Saverne, called "Tres Tabernae" during the Roman period, is situated at the foot of the Vosges where the valley which links Lorraine to the Alsatian plain opens out.

The parish church, whose oldest part, the 12th century bell tower decorated with the characteristic "lésènes" and Lombard bands, was built in the 14th century and reconstructed in the 15th and 16th centuries. It contains some very beautiful furnishings, especially 15th and 16th century sculptures.

Saverne also still has several old houses of great beauty, in particular those either side of the Town Hall. One of these, no. 80 Grand' Rue which dates from 1605, is notable for its carved beams, its oriel supported by a stone console, and its half-timbered front finely decorated with a four-membered motif.

However Saverne was also the residence of the Prince-Bishops of Strasbourg. Two fires, in 1708 and in 1779, destroyed the parts of the castle rebuilt first by Coysevox and then later by Robert de Cotte. The present castle was reconstructed in 1779-1790 by Salins de Montfort for Count Louis de Rohan. The long façade overlooking the garden, with its projecting parts and the rhythmical feeling imparted by the columns and pillars, is characteristic of that search for monumentality inspired by classical models which distinguished the end of the 18th century.

Saverne: the parish church.

Saverne: the Castle.

Saverne: a typical ▶ house in Grand'Rue.

HAUT-BARR

Haut-Barr, the ancient fortress of the Prince-Bishops of Strasbourg, dominates the plain. Great blocks of sandstone hewn out of the site itself were used to construct the base. The oldest extant part is the 12th century chapel whose walls are decorated with Lombard bands.

The castle was enlarged and transformed in 1580-86 by Jean de Manderscheid, the Bishop of Strasbourg.

Haut-Barr: the Castle.

STRASBOURG

Thanks to its position at the meeting of several rivers, the site on which Strasbourg now stands has been inhabited since the Bronze Age. During the Roman period, "Argentoratum", as it was then called, became important mainly as a frontier town facing the Germanic tribes not yet under Roman domination. It was completely destroyed by Attila, but after the battle of Tolbiac in 496 a rebuilt town which came to be known as "Stratiburgum" rose from the ruins. After about 1100 the town grew up rapidly thanks to the energy of an enterprising middle class. In 1262 they freed themselves from the control of the bishop who had been the highest authority for a very long time. The 14th century was marked by growing prosperity, with the building of the Customs House and the first bridge over the Rhine, all of which made Strasbourg a major centre for trade in northern Europe. In order to gain the support of the city successive emperors granted it a series of privileges and customs exemptions which in practice made it independent of the Empire. This culminated in the city declaring itself a free republic in the 15th century. In the 16th century it became both a centre for the diffusion of the ideas of the Reformation and thanks to the presence of a number of great Protestant thinkers as well as Swiss, French and Italian Protestants to whom it had offered refuge, a Protestant cultural centre.

Its political decline started at the end of the 16th century and was finally sealed by the annexation of the Republic of Strasbourg to the Kingdom of France in 1697. This opened a new chapter in the history of the city. The links with France brought about a rapid development of its prosperity and of its social and cultural life. In the 18th and 19th centuries the political events which occupied the city were the same as those which occupied the rest of France: the Revolution (in 1792 Rouget de l'Isle sung the Marseillaise, later to become the national anthem, for the first time), Napoleon and the Empire, the Restoration and finally Napoleon III and the Second Empire. The defeat of the Second Empire in the Franco-Prussian War had serious consequences both for Strasbourg and for Alsace as a whole. In 1870, after six weeks of bombardment, the city was annexed to the New German Empire as the capital of the Empire's new region Alsace-Lorraine. It was only in 1918, at the end of the First World War, that the city was once again reunited with

Panoramic view of Strasbourg.

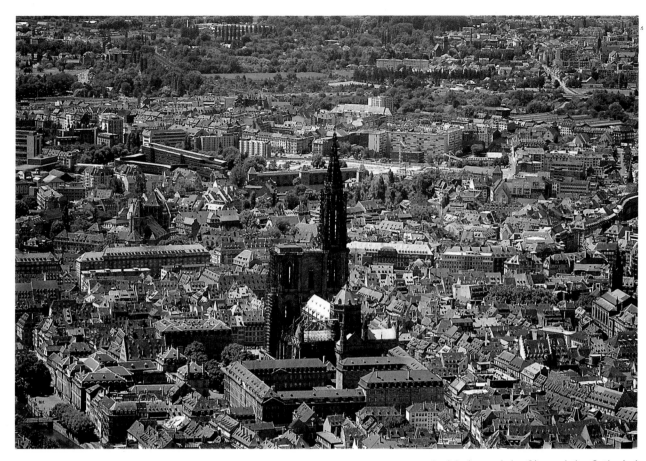

Aerial views of the City and the Cathedral.

France, from which however, in its heart, it had never been separated. In the Second World War Strasbourg was badly hit. In 1940 the Nazis annexed Alsace. The Allied bombardment of the city during August and September 1944 caused numerous victims and widespread destruction. In the post-war period Strasbourg regained that European dimension which it had during the golden centuries of its history. In 1949 it was chosen to be the site for the Council of Europe and since 1979 it has been the seat of the European Parliament.

THE CATHEDRAL

The cathedral, referred to as "le grand ange rose de Strasbourg" (the great pink angel of Strasbourg) by Paul Claudel, is one of the most remarkable masterpieces of Gothic art in northern Europe. The streets of the old city centre are dominated by this tremendous building with its architecturally bold design. The first church of Our Lady on this site, which would have been a wooden construction, was built round about 510 A.D.. However in a document dated 826 A.D. the

Carolingian basilica is described as being built of stone with two apses, one at the east end and one at the west end, and a crypt. After a fire this first cathedral was demolished and replaced by an imposing basilica started in 1015 by Bishop Wernher. The present building has retained the layout of the choir of this basilica. Following another major fire in 1176 Bishop Conrad of Hünebourg decided to rebuild the east end and the transept. This rebuilding took place in four stages finishing in 1240. While the choir, the crossing of the transept and the

16

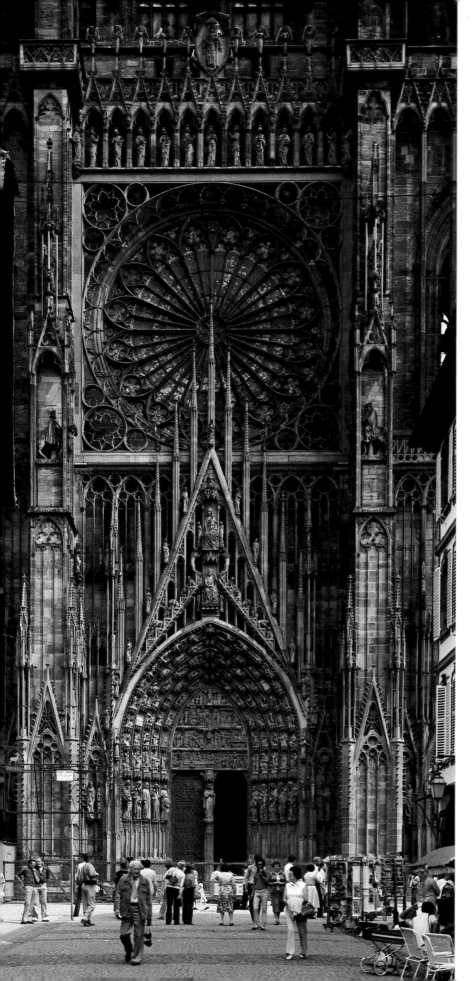

north wing of the transept are still very much in the Romanesque tradition, the workshop which took over the construction of the south wing of the transept in 1225 had a distinctly Gothic conception of space and in its decorative work it clearly showed architectural influences originating in the Ile-de-France. From 1240 onwards yet another workshop was responsible for the construction of the nave which was built in the purest Gothic style. They used French construction techniques but managed to retain a Germanic character thanks to the great arches opening on to the aisles, a triforium decorated with openwork which gives onto the high windows filled with stained and to the great piers whose complex structure corresponds to that of the ribbed vaulting. The west end or narthex is the work of Erwin of Steinbach. A romantic myth has grown up about this architect which continues to be associated with the cathedral. In 1365 the façade at the west end was finished up to the level of the platform. In 1384 Michael of Fribourg built the belfry above which rises the majestic spire which was completed in 1439.

The façade

When you emerge from the Rue Mercière into the cathedral square you receive the full impact of the enormous façade which manages to be both grandiose (it is 66 metres high and 45 metres wide) and yet amazingly delicate. It was under construction from 1277 to 1365. At the beginning of the 15th century the architect of Ulm cathedral, Ulrich of Ensingen, built the octagonal part of the tower. The spire which soars to 142 metres was finally finished in 1439 by John Hultz of Cologne.

The three richly decorated doorways use a complex imagery which was undoubtedly inspired by Albert the Great. Many statues which were damaged during the Reformation or the French Revolution have been restored or copies made and some

The Cathedral: centre doorway on the west side.

The Cathedral: Christ and the Wise Virgins (detail of the centre doorway).

are now to be found in the cathedral museum (Museé de l'Œuvre Notre-Dame). The left-hand door is dedicated to the Childhood of Christ and on the jambs the Virtues pierce the Vices with their lances. In the centre door on the jambs are huge figures of the Prophets while the tympanum shows scenes from the Passion and the door is crowned by a gable on which are enthroned first Solomon then the Virgin and Child beneath the head of God the Father. Along the sides of the gable are twelve lions representing the twelve tribes of Israel. In the right-hand door the tympanum shows the Last Judgement while in the jambs the Wise Virgins stand with Christ and the Foolish Virgins stand with the Tempter. All this work was carried out between 1280 and 1300 and although it was done in a typically Rhenish style the influence of Paris and Rheims are clearly visible. Over the centre door is the magnificent openwork rosewindow flanked by the equestrian statues of the Merovingian and Carolingian Kings, with above it a gallery. Just beneath the platform can be seen high relief figures representing the Last Judgement.

The south door

The doorway in the south transept is particularly interesting. The two female figures on the right and the left of the doorway, which were carved between 1225 and 1235 but which have now been replaced by copies, are allegorical representations of the Synagogue and the Church Triumphant, the latter being more solemn and having an almost virile grace. The two tympana which depict respectively the Death and the Coronation of the Virgin are considered to be among the great masterpieces of French 13th century sculpture.

The interior

Built in a relatively short period of time (1236-1275) the nave is a perfect example of Gothic art. It is the masterpiece of an anonymous architect who freely interpreted and

The Cathedral: doorway in the south transept.

The Cathedral: the interior. ▶

The Cathedral: the pulpit.

The Cathedral: a stained glass window.

blended the models provided by the great cathedrals of the Ile-de-France, Champagne and Burgundy. The construction of the nave started at the east end and continued west by following the perimeter of the Romanesque basilica. This accounts for the exceptional width of the aisles, for a Gothic church, and explains the unusual one to two ratio of width to height which results in a less marked verticality than in other Gothic cathedrals in the North of France.

The pulpit

The superb pulpit about halfway down the nave was built round about 1485 by Hans Hammer for Prior Geiler of Kaysersberg. Round the bottom are statues representing the four Evangelists and the Fathers of the Church, while round the central pillar are carved a Virgin and Child, St. Catherine, St. Barbe, a bishop and an unknown saint. In the upper part is a Christ on the

Cross flanked by the Apostles. Underneath the stairs is a scene from the legend of St. Alexis.

The stained glass windows

In the words of Paul Claudel Strasbourg cathedral "raconte à travers ses vitraux tous les siècles, toute l'histoire profane et sacrée" (by means of its stained glass it tells the story of every century and retails its history both sacred and

profane). Throughout the church, in the choir, the transept, the nave and the side chapels, the stained glass windows are intimately linked to the history of the building and constitute a subtle complement to the architecture and the sculpture. Starting off relatively small, the windows occupy practically the whole of the walls by the time we get to the nave and the aisles, and in this way open up the inside of the church to the light. The stained glass was manufactured in various workshops. The iconographic themes are also very varied. In the North transept the windows depict the Judgement of Solomon while in the South transept the great rose-windows illustrate scenes from the Old and New Testaments. In the nave the tall windows represent various saints, both male and female, those in the triforium the ancestors of Christ, those in the north aisle various emperors, and those in the south aisle the life of the Virgin and the life of Christ. Finally the great rose-window at the West End combines its finely carved tracery with a geometric design.

The organ

The organ was built at the end of the 15th century by Frederick Krebs using an older console dating from 1385. It was modified by André Silbermann at the beginning of the 18th century. The console is decorated with polychrome wood sculptures: four angel musicians, Samson taming the lion, and two figures known as "Rohraffcn", one blowing into a trumpet and the other representing a pretzel seller. In fact they are two large articulated marionettes, which were worked by a person hidden inside who was also the voice of the "Rohraffe". The "Rohraffe" satirised the prior to such an extent that the celebrated Geiser of Kaysersberg took the matter up with the courts but without obtaining satisfaction.

The Cathedral: the organ.

The angel pillar

Situated in the centre of the south transept, the Angel Pillar also called the Last Judgement Pillar is one of the marvels of the cathedral, combining as it does a precise architectural function with a decorative and iconographic function. At the bottom are the four evangelists with their symbols, next come four angel musicians and finally the enthroned Christ with three angels bringing him the instruments of the Passion. Executed ca. 1235-1240 by an anonymous artist referred to as "the first Gothic master" these elegant figures remind us of the great statuary of Chartres.

The astronomical clock

The astronomical clock which dominates the south transept is the work of art which most perfectly embodies the spirit of the Renaissance in Strasbourg. Intended to replace a previous 14th century clock, work on it was begun in 1547. After an interruption, work was continued from 1571 to 1574 by a new team consisting of the mathematician Dasypodius, the brothers Habrecht who were clockmakers, the architect Hans Uhlberger and the painter Tobias Stimmer, who not only decorated it but also made the models for the sculptures. Between 1838 and 1842 J.B. Schwilgué replaced the very complicated mechanisms. On the quarter hours Christ chases away Death, represented by a skeleton, who is only allowed to strike on the hour. The quarter hours are struck by small allegorical figures representing the Four Ages of Man. At midday the Apostles pass before Christ and bow their heads to receive his blessing while at the same time a cock spreads its wings and crows. At the end of this daily performance Christ turns towards the crowd and blesses it.

The Cathedral: the Angel Pillar.

The Cathedral: view of the ▶ astronomical clock.

PHARMACIE DU CERF (THE HART PHARMACY)

The Pharmacie du Cerf, which is directly opposite the cathedral, is one of the oldest in Europe. In the course of its history, which goes back seven centuries, it has had many famous clients including Goethe, who often came from his nearby house at 36 rue du Vieux-Marché-aux-Poissons to chat with his friend, the pharmacist Spielmann. Already in existence in 1262, the pharmacy was rebuilt in the 15th century. The vaulted arches on the ground floor are decorated with the sculpted vegetation characteristic of this period. The upper floors with the half-timbering so typical of Alsatian architecture were finished in 1567.

KAMMERZELL HOUSE

Among the many picturesque dwellings in the cathedral square this one stands out by its massive wooden construction and its pointed gable. An earlier 15th century building, whose stone-built ground floor has been incorporated into the present one, was purchased in 1571 by Martin Braun, a rich textile merchant. He commissioned the building of the upper stories which are richly decorated with wood carvings representing the Signs of the Zodiac, the five senses, the Four Ages of Man, and the heroes of classical antiquity and medieval legends who were so much in vogue during the Renaissance. Over the years the ownership of the house changed many times but it always

retained its commercial function (on the west side you can still see the winch used to hoist goods up to the loft) until in 1879 a grocer called Kammerzell sold it to the Œuvre Notre-Dame (the cathedral's Board of Commissioners). In 1892 a complete restoration partially changed the external appearance of the house by the addition of polychrome paintings in the style of 16th century Rhenish artists. For many years now, the inside has housed a restaurant serving local specialities. In 1910 a fresco illustrating a famous "culinary" episode in the history of Strasbourg was painted by Léo Schnugg. In 1576 a boat arrived from Zurich after 18 hours on the river and presented the city with a pot of still-warm soup, in order to prove to

The Place du Marché-aux-cochons-de-lait.

◄ *Cathedral Square with the Pharmacie du Cerf (left) and the Kammerzell House (right, background).*

the people of Strasbourg that their allies from Zurich could come to their help extremely quickly. The fragments of this pot are still preserved in the historical museum (Musée historique).

PLACE DU MARCHE-AUX-COCHONS-DE-LAIT

Formerly the market-place where piglets were bought and sold, this square has preserved its 17th and 18th century buildings almost intact. The most famous building in the square is no. 1 which has the

half-timbering typical of Alsatian houses, as well as external galleries of the type very commonly found in country houses in the region but rarely found in town houses. Put up in 1617 over a stone-built ground floor at least two centuries older, it was still a part of that golden age of timbered Strasbourg architecture which flourished in the second half of the 16th century. On the top a boot shaped weather vane recalls a legendary episode of local history. In 1414 the emperor Sigismund was invited to a ball by the ladies of the town. He arrived somewhat the worse for wear after a long tramp through the snow. The kind-hearted ladies took pity on him and immediately rushed out and bought him a good pair of boots from the boot-maker who had his shop at no. 1.

CHATEAU ROHAN

This princely residence of Strasbourg's bishops was built between 1731 and 1742 at the instigation of Armand Gaston de Rohan-Soubise, whose family occupied the bishopric throughout the 18th century. By feudal tradition the bishop was also the Landgrave of Lower Alsace and an Imperial Prince. The architect Robert de Cotte created an imposing complex of buildings arranged around a square courtyard. The main façade, the centre of which was occupied by four large Corinthian columns, looks over the river Ill. The north façade which looks onto the Place du Château consists of two buildings joined by the gateway of honour which is decorated with allegorical statues by Robert de Lorrain. Access to the sumptuous state apartments ("Grands Appartements") inspired by those of Versailles and intended for public functions, and to the more intimate and comfortable living quarters ("Petits Appartements") decorated in a delicate Rococo style, is from the courtyard. Among the many famous people who have stayed in the Château was King Louis XV who, together with his wife Maria Lezczynska, spent a period of convalescence here. On that occasion great festivities were organised and the buildings oppo-

site were hidden from view by a huge canvas in trompe-l'œil depicting gardens in perspective. In 1770 Marie-Antoinette, future Queen of France, stayed here for a short while. In 1805 Napoleon, who had been given the château by the city of Strasbourg, also stayed here. It was badly damaged by bombing in 1944 but has since been completely restored. It now houses the Musée des Beaux-Arts (Fine Art Gallery), the Musée Archéologique (Archeo-logical Museum), and the Musée des Arts Décoratifs (Museum of Decorative Arts). The latter is famed for its splendid collections of pottery, decorated earthenware and porcelain and in particular those from the potteries of Hannong, Strasbourg and Haguenau. The Musée des Beaux-Arts which is on the first and second floors contains Flemish, Dutch, Italian and Spanish painting from the 14th to the 19th centuries.

Château Rohan: the façade seen from the Ill.

THE MUSEUM OF MODERN ART

Opened in 1965 the museum occupies the old Customs House which was built in 1358. It was enlarged in the 16th century and then rebuilt after the last war. The main artistic movements of the last 100 years are all represented in the collection. Among the exhibits are works by the Impressionists, Paul Gauguin, Paul Klee, Raoul Dufy and Georges Braque. Perhaps the best known painting is "The Kiss", a large preparatory study by Gustav Klimt for the decoration of the interior of Stoclet House in Brussels. One whole room is devoted to projects and drawings by the Strasbourg artist Jean Arp (1877-1966) who had links with both the "Blaue Reiter" (Blue Rider) group and the Dada movement.

PLACE GUTENBERG

Known up until 1781 as the "Marché aux Herbes" (Vegetable Market), this square was in fact the economic and administrative centre of the city from the Middle Ages until the Revolution. It was also the spot where the great events in local life took place. The festivities organised in 1682 to celebrate the birth of King Louis XV have remained a legend. The solemn building which houses the Chamber of Commerce, finished in 1585 and intended to accommodate the merchants' associations on the ground floor and the city administration on the upper floors, is a reminder of the former splendour of the square. The façade is particularly fine with its superimposed orders and the extremely elegant and finely sculpted decoration. The architect is unknown. In the middle of the square is the bronze statue of Gutenberg executed by the sculptor David d'Angers in 1840 to celebrate the fourth centenary of the invention of printing using moveable type. It was in Strasbourg between 1433 and 1445 that Gutenberg perfected his invention with the help of a jeweller and a carpenter. Gutenberg is shown in a standing position beside a printing press. Round the base four reliefs illustrate the benefits to mankind of this great invention.

THE COUR DU CORBEAU

This old inn (the Crow Inn), built in 1528 and which continued in use until 1854, is to be found at no. 1 Quai des Bateliers, whose name means Boatsmen's Wharf. The 16th and 17th century buildings of the Crow Inn, built of wood in the architectural style of the region, give onto a splendid courtyard.

◄ *The Museum of Modern Art.*

Gutenberg Square (or Place Gutenberg) with the monument.

ST. THOMAS' CHURCH

Built between the 12th and the 15th centuries in an austere Gothic style, its size makes it the city's most important church after the cathedral and one of the most important churches in Alsace. The original layout with five naves of equal height has been modified appreciably only in the apse, in order to accomodate the funerary monument of Maurice de Saxe, the masterpiece of the sculptor J.B. Pigalle. Louis XV's valliant general enters the tomb which Death has opened for him while France tries to restrain him. A Hercules in tears represents the Army's grief, and the animals on the tomb are the heraldic personifications of the countries he defeated in battle: England, Holland and the Holy Roman Empire.

PLACE DE L'HOMME-DE-FER

The former charm of this square, known in the Middle Ages as the Square of the Two Lime Trees, is largely gone due mainly to the destruction caused by the last war. The 18th century building to which it

St. Thomas' church:
Maurice de Saxe's funerary monument.

Place de l'Homme-de-Fer with the famous Tram.

owes its name still exists at no. 2. From 1740 to 1870 it was a gunsmith's shop whose sign was an "homme de fer" (man of iron), a life-size model of a sergeant of the city militia dressed in 15th century armour. A replica of the "iron man" is still in its original place.

PLACE KLEBER

Together with the cathedral square this is one of the places dearest to the hearts of the people of Strasbourg. It was here that the military parades of the Ancien Régime, the great events of the French Revolution, and the festivities celebrating the end of the two world wars all took place. It was because of the "military" role which the square has played all through the history of Strasbourg that it was chosen as the burial place for the ashes of General Kléber. They were placed beneath the bronze statue executed in 1840 by Philippe Grass. Napoleon's famous general, a

Place Kléber: General Kléber's statue.

The model by Pierre Zanuttini showing the future appearance of Place Kléber.

A view of the Petite France district.

native of Strasbourg, died during the Egyptian campaign in 1800. At the request of his fellow citizens his ashes were returned to the city, so that they could give an honourable burial to their hero who symbolized Strasbourg's ties to France.

In 1940 the statue was removed by the Nazis who transferred the general's mortal remains to the Cronenbourg military cemetery.

In 1945 they were restored to their rightful place under the statue, round whose base bronze reliefs commemorate the battles of Altenkirchen and Heliopolis.

LA PETITE FRANCE

The oldest part of the medieval centre of the city is situated to the west of the Roman part. It corresponds to the first and third enlargements of the medieval city which took place respectively round about 1100 and between 1228 and 1334. Petite France, formerly the district inhabited by millers, fishermen and tanners, is among the most evocative and the best preserved in the whole city, in spite of the changes which on several occasions, in 1912 and again in 1930-36 in particular,

have irrevocably changed its appearance. The name Petite France which has come to mean the whole of the tanners district is derived from the name of the quay which runs along the characteristic rue des Moulins. Soldiers of the armies of Charles VIII and Louis XII returning from the Italian campaigns suffering from venereal diseases were treated at no. 2 of this quay, which came to be known as "Zum Französel" (the Italians called venereal diseases "the French sickness" "*mal francese*" or "*francioso*" while the French called it "the

Petite France: the Tanners' House.

Italian sickness" or the "Neapolitan sickness"). Rue des Moulins joins the square of the same name to rue du Bain-aux-Plantes where the Tanners' Corporation was formerly to be found. Although the mania for modernisation has not spared this street, formerly one of the most picturesque in "Old Strasbourg", it still has some interesting 16th and 17th century buildings, connected with the work of the tanneries which occupied an important position in the flourishing commercial activities of the city. In these houses, whose artisanal activity ceased during the last century, the hides were tanned and then dried on wattle grids made from reeds grown for this purpose on the banks of the river Ill. The tannin once dried was recovered and used as a cheap fuel called "Lohkaes". This is also the name of the tanners' ancient tavern, a wood and stone construction dating from the end of the 16th century at no. 25 of the same street. Of the same period and style, the "Tanners' House" at no. 24 has a beautiful façade with galleries one above the other overlooking the river Ill.

The Palais du Rhin
or Rhine Palace.

St. Paul's church ▶

THE RHINE PALACE (PALAIS DU RHIN)

After the annexation of Strasbourg by the German Empire in 1870 the Place de la République, dominated by the massive triumphal architecture of the Imperial Palace, became the hub of the new city.

Built between 1883 and 1889 by the architect Hermann Hegert in the style of Berlin public buildings, the palace is clearly inspired by Florentine Renaissance architecture of which it has adopted the rough hewn stone facings known as rustication. A huge balcony in the form of a classical temple projects from the centre of the main façade.

The palace is capped by an imposing cupola covering the central part of the monumental staircase leading up to the ballroom and the Imperial apartments on the first floor. Unfortunately, following the bombing in 1944 little remains of the original luxurious decoration. At the present time the Palace, which changed its name to the Palais du Rhin after Alsace-Lorraine was returned to France in 1918, houses various cultural organisations.

ST. PAUL'S CHURCH

The so-called "German Town", which was intentionally built in an area separate from the old part of the city in order to emphasize the German cultural impact on the recently annexed territory, is today perfectly integrated into Strasbourg's urban structure, largely as a result of the dynamic post-war development. The architects Orth and Conrath drew up a plan for the urban development of the district with the intention that it should become the political and administrative centre of Strasbourg. Wide regular streets linked the imposing public buildings concentrated in this area. They reflected the architectural eclecticism in vogue at the end of the 19th century. An excellent example is the Protestant church of St. Paul, built in 1892 in neo-Gothic style using as its model the church of St. Elizabeth in Marburg.

THE PALACE OF EUROPE (LE PALAIS DE L'EUROPE)

In the immediate post-war period, when the major West European nations had agreed on the need for European union, Strasbourg was chosen as the headquarters for the Council of Europe and this was officially accepted in 1949. In 1950 in the period when the city, under the leadership of the mayor, Charles Frey, was occupied in its own reconstruction after the severe damage inflicted on it during the war, the first buildings intended for the Council of Europe started to go up opposite the park known as l'Orangerie. The last building built in this new "international" Strasbourg was the Palace of Europe (Palais de l'Europe) designed by the architect Henry Bernard and finished in 1976. This huge complex, housing the vast chamber of the European Parliament and its numerous offices, is a complete break with the conformism of most modern architecture. Inside the great square building resembling some futuristic fortress, the semi-circular chamber covered by a daring transparent dome looks like nothing so much as a great vitrified shell. It is here that the sittings of the European Parliament in existence as a directly elected body since 1979 (after a long gestation of nearly 30 years) take place.

Interior of the Palace of Europe.

MOLSHEIM

Molsheim is still partly surrounded by its city wall. The Metzig or Old Meat Market in the Place de l'Hôtel de Ville (Town Hall Square) is a living witness to the wealth of the town in the 16th century. This vast building is rectangular in shape and its sides are topped by large voluted gables. It was on the ground floor that the meat was actually displayed. On the front of the building, which faces the square, two sets of stairs, rising one from the left and one from the right, meet under a small clock-tower and give access to the first floor whose windows open onto a balcony. The original clock with mechanical figures was replaced in the 17th century by the present arrangement in which angels sound the hours and the quarter hours. There are three quadrants marking the hours, the quarter hours and the phases of the moon. The whole thing is crowned with a niche containing a statue of the Virgin and Child which also dates from the 17th century.

At the end of the 16th century, Strasbourg having become a major centre of the Reformation, its cathedral Chapter decided to move to Molsheim. In 1580 the Jesuits founded a college here and then in 1677 a Faculty of Philosophy and Theology. In this way Molsheim became a refuge for catholicism until 1702, the year in which Louis XV had the Faculty transferred back to Strasbourg. This is the context in which we must see the construction between 1609 and 1618 of the Jesuit church. It was designed by Christophe Wamser, the architect of the Jesuit church in Cologne, in a style marrying the Gothic and Renaissance traditions. The stucco decoration by Jean Kuhn dates from 1632.

Molsheim: the old Meat Market ("Metzig").

ROSHEIM

Situated in the midst of hilly country the small town of Rosheim still has part of its city walls including the four gateways, one of which has been incorporated into the Town Hall. In the square there is a well with a stone canopy over it dating from 1632. After being burnt down in 1132 by the troops of the Duke of Swabia the town, now under the protection of Frederick of Hohenstaufen, was rebuilt. Apart from the city walls the other structure which has survived from the 12th century is the only remaining Romanesque house in Alsace, commonly known, though without any historical foundation, as the Maison des Païens (House of the Pagans). The upper floor still has its chimney. The twin window on the front is decorated with masks.

The church of St. Peter-and-St. Paul is one of the most beautiful Romanesque churches in Alsace. It may have been built at the request of Frederick Barbarossa. The only thing remaining of the original church is the two-level choir tower, lying somewhat to the south of the choir of the present church which was built between 1150 and 1170. However it is the decorative sculpture which is of particular interest in this church. It was the first use in Alsace of sculpture in the round, with carved figures being placed on the crossing tower and in the nave and the transept. But the sculptured

*Rosheim: a detail of
House of the Pagans' façade.*

*Rosheim:
St. Peter-and-Paul's church.*

Rosheim: the ancient pulley-well. ▶

decoration extends to the bas-reliefs, such as the tetramorphs on either side of the window in the choir.

The doors and windows are similarly surrounded by a profusion of decorative detail. They are usually flanked by twin columns decorated with billets (short rolls inserted at intervals in the hollow molding), checks, or palmleaves.

The façades are full of modillions (projecting brackets under a cornice) and friezes. The overall impression of perfection and clarity which emanates from this building is due as much to the balance between the architecture and the decorative sculpture as to the quality of the cutting of the stone.

OBERNAI

Obernai is a picturesque small town very well known for the important and very popular festival held every year to celebrate the marriage of Friend Fritz (l'Ami Fritz). Founded by the Romans, in the 7th century Obernai became the main residence of Duke Adalric or Etichon, Duke of Alsace and father of the future St. Odile, who went on to found the convent of Hohenberg (in fact it was a gift from her father who after first persecuting her recognized the error of his ways). There is a 19th century statue of St. Odile in the middle of the Place du Marché (Market Place) commemorating her place of birth.

Obernai: a view of Place de l'Etoile. ▶

Obernai: Market Place ▶
(Place du Marché) and the Halle aux blés.

Obernai: panoramic view.

In the 16th century a double fortified wall was built round the town and it still encloses the main part of the town. It is now planted with lime trees. Most of the more important monuments date from the 16th century, in particular the very beautiful Place du Marché.

The Corn Exchange with its high gable dates from 1554. On the other side of the square the Hôtel de Ville or Town Hall, the work of Hans Jüngling, was built at the beginning of the 16th century. The large Council Chamber on the first floor was decorated with murals illustrating the Ten Commandments in the 17th century and was further embellished in 1604 by the addition of a stone balcony and an oriel. The man who carried out these improvements, Georges Widemann, a native of Strasbourg, also added a gallery with four small open-work stone towers and a spire to the "Kappelturm", which is now the belfry of the Town Hall but was formerly the bell tower of a 13th century chapel. Either side of the square, around the neo-Gothic late 19th century church, old half-timbered houses, often with high gables, line the narrow streets and small squares.

The well, known as the Puits aux Six Sceaux (well with six seals), dates from 1579 and is the work of two Strasbourg artisans, Henri Ottmann and Conrad Miller. Its wall is divided into panels each with a decorative rose in the centre. Three columns essentially Corinthian in style support a stone canopy carrying various inscriptions in a series of cartouches. The whole thing is roofed over in zinc.

Obernai: the Well with Six Seals (Puits aux Six Sceaux).　　　*Obernai: an ancient oriel in the Market Place.*

44

MONT SAINTE-ODILE

Mont Sainte-Odile is the Holy Mountain of Alsace and overlooks the plain above Obernai. The convent is built on top of a sandstone platform. After the death of St. Odile the convent of Hohenberg became a centre of pilgrimage and was renamed after the saint.

The 12th century, which was the golden age for Alsace, was also an exceptional period for the convent. Frederick Barbarossa stayed there in 1153 and appointed one of his relatives, Relinde, as abbess. Later it was here that the abbess Herade of Landsberg wrote one of the most important 12th century Rhenish works, the "Hortus Deliciarum", a

Sainte-Odile: St. Odile's statue in the cloister.

Sainte-Odile: aerial view.

general survey of theology combining the ideas of the period with evocations of the courtly life of the Middle Ages. Unfortunately the manuscript itself was destroyed in the fire at the Bibliothèque Nationale in Strasbourg in 1870, and only copies survive.

The convent itself was almost entirely destroyed by fire in 1546 and only a few vestiges from the Romanesque period have survived. Most of the buildings were rebuilt in the 17th and 18th centuries and redecorated in the 20th century. For example the mosaic in the Chapelle des Anges (Angels' Chapel) dates from only 1947.

In St. John's chapel there is a very beautiful lintel from round about 1050 representing a tree of life. The vaulting in the chapel of the Cross is supported by a central column decorated with palm leaves and grotesques. The Chapel of Tears, in the north east corner of the terrace, was built over a Merovingian cemetery.

Sainte-Odile:
St. Odile Chapel's interior.

Sainte-Odile: the Chapel of Tears
(Chapelle des Larmes).

Sainte-Odile: view of the mosaic
in the Angels' Chapel.

THE PAGAN WALL

On the slopes of Mont Sainte-Odile the forest of the Vosges, full of firs, chestnut trees and beeches, extends as far as the eye can see.

A puzzling vestige of the past, the Pagan Wall extends for more than 10 kilometres and encloses over 100 hectares of forest.

Even though the origin of this wall is not known with any certainty — is it from the pre-Roman period or is it late Roman? — one cannot but be impressed by the quality of its construction, the gigantic blocks of stone being held together by wooden dove-tails.

Church of Sainte-Odile: the exterior.

Sainte-Odile: the Pagan Wall.

BARR

An important centre of Alsatian wine growing and the site of the annual Alsatian Wine Fair together with the traditional celebrations which accompany it, Barr has developed into a gastronomic and touristic centre as well. Built on the hills and surrounded by vineyards, the upper part of the town is dominated by the church which still has its Romanesque bell tower. The different levels of the bell tower are decorated with "lésènes" and Lombard bands, a style of decoration very common in Alsace.

The main street leads up to the Place de l'Hôtel de Ville (Town Hall Square) with its fountain and its old houses which, because of the sloping terrain, are built on terraces. A huge stairway leads down to the half-timbered houses and narrow streets, of the lower town.

The Town Hall was built in 1640 over older foundations. The ground floor has a series of arches. In the

middle of the façade there is an oriel resting on stone modillions (a kind of stone bracket). Above the oriel is a balcony and a pediment, decorated with convex and concave curves, which projects from the steep roof and is crowned with a small belfry.

By the north exit of the town, right in the middle of the vineyards, is Marco's Folie, built for Louis Felix Marco, the Council's barrister and the bailiff of the domain of the lord of Barr during the second half of the 18th century. This beautiful house has now been converted into a museum. Distinguishing outside features are two porches each topped with a balcony, the curved projecting central part and the garden, while the inside is noted for the three reception rooms, one above the other, and the library.

Barr: Hôtel Restaurant Le Brochet.

Barr, the Town Hall Square: the fountain and the Town Hall.

SELESTAT

Sélestat although belonging to the group of towns in the foothills of the Vosges is sufficiently in the plain to find itself on the main north-south axis of communications of Alsace. From its past it has retained a collection of works of art and items of historical interest which warrant an attention too often denied them by Sélestat's proximity to Strasbourg.

It is known that Charlemagne stayed here in 775 and the existence of a port joined to the river Ill testifies to commercial activity very early on. However it is rather through its religious history that Sélestat has been marked by the Middle Ages and the Renaissance. At the end of the 11th century Hildegarde of Eguisheim who had built a "church on the model of the Holy Sepulchre" decided to found a Benedictine monastery nearby. The monks who filled the first great monastic centre in Sélestat and who, half a century later, built the Sainte-Foy Basilica, came from the Abbey, organised around the tomb of Sainte Foy, at Conques in Rouergue.

Some features of civic architecture, but above all two great medieval churches, together with the treasures of the humanist library, constitute the most important vestiges from the past. The ancient convent church of Sainte-Foy has some of the characteristics of other Romanesque churches in Alsace. However other influences can be seen in the building and the rhythm imparted to the external masses by the two towers of the façade and the octagonal crossing tower suggest Burgundy.

Not far away the former parish church of Our Lady, which became St. George's at the end of the Middle Ages, provides an example of Gothic architecture. The westend, built in the 14th century, and the central nave and its aisles, built in the 13th century, lead into a long rectangular choir, very imaginative in design, built (about 1400-1420) to replace the previous choir.

Sélestat: the Church of Sainte-Foy.

Sélestat: St. George's church.

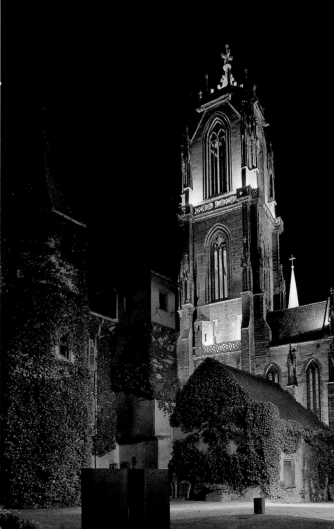

Haut-Kœnigsbourg: aerial view.

THE HAUT-KŒNIGSBOURG

The castle of the Haut-Kœnigsbourg is built on a rocky platform rising up more than 720 metres from the Plain of Alsace to the south west of Sélestat. In the 12th century two castles separated by a wide moat, each with a square keep, were built there. The succession to the lordship during the 13th and 14th centuries was much disputed being coveted in particular by the Dukes of Lorraine and the Bishops of Strasbourg. Lorraine only renounced its rights to the lordship in 1474.

In 1454 it was besieged by Count Palatin. In 1462 it was almost completely destroyed after being used by a band of brigands who ransomed noblemen and merchants. It remained a ruin until 1479 when it was rebuilt by the Counts of Thierstein and the ruins which have been restored date largely from this period. From 1519 to 1533 the castle was entrusted to military governors, then it was pledged and

passed into the hands of the Sickingen family but, inhabited only by a provost, it was practically allowed to run to ruin. In 1606 Rodolphe of Bollwiller had the defences rebuilt. At his death it was in the hands of the Counts of Fugger.

In 1633 the castle was besieged by a party of Swedes and after a siege of several months Philippe de Lichtenau, the commander of the fortress, surrendered. The castle was burnt down. Louis XIV, having become by the Treaty of Westphalia the sovereign of the province of Alsace in 1648, took the castle from the Fuggers and gave it back to the Sickingen family. They sold it in 1770 to the President of the Sovereign Council of Alsace, a man called Bourg who kept the ruins until 1865. In 1865 after many changes of ownership it was finally bought by the town of Sélestat who gave it to Emperor William II at the time of an official visit in 1899.

William II wanted to revitalize the Haut-Kœnigsbourg and decided, in spite of strong opposition, to rebuild the castle. The work was started in 1900 under the supervi-

Haut-Kœnigsbourg: the Castle.

sion of Bodo Ebhardt, an architect who had already restored a large number of fortresses in Germany. The bulk of the work was finished in 1908. It is important to stress that this was not the restoration of a medieval castle but a reconstruction based much more on the architect's and the emperor's conception of the Middle Ages than on archeological realities. The machicoulis, the brattices and the massive square keep with its embossments suggest the Neo-Gothic style of the end of the 19th or beginning of the 20th century rather than medieval military architecture. The interior was also entirely refitted. The murals are the work of Leo Schnug. The furniture, wainscoting and panelling, the arms and armour, and the other elements of the décor are also very typical of the period both in the taste for the monumental and in the mixture of styles.

The castle of the Haut-Kœnigsbourg which was returned to France in 1919 is now maintained by the Caisse Nationale des Monuments Historiques.

Haut-Kœnigsbourg: ▶
Knights' Hall.

Haut-Kœnigsbourg: ▶
Banqueting Room.

Kintzheim: the Castle.

Ribeauvillé: the Butchers' Tower ▶
(Tour des Bouchers).

KINTZHEIM

Kintzheim castle in the Bas-Rhin not far from Sélestat (not to be confused with Kintzheim, a little town near Colmar) is linked to the history of the noble family of Rathsamhausen. In plan it is a large rectangular ensemble containing various buildings. The façades facing the plain contain numerous windows and the circular keep overlooks all. Birds of prey, used for giving spectacular demonstrations, are raised here, which shows the uses to which these medieval castles, often set in splendid natural sites, can be put.

RIBEAUVILLE

At the foot of the famous castles of Girsberg, Saint-Ulrich and Haut-Ribeaupierre, Ribeauvillé has preserved the charm of by-gone days. It still celebrates "Pfifferdag", the day of the wandering fiddlers who, in times gone by, used to pay homage to the lord of Ribeaupierre on the first Sunday in September.

The Grand'Rue is lined with old houses and the squares have fountains, such as the one in front of the 18th century Town Hall. Built in 1536 it is decorated with a lion bearing the arms of William I of Ribeaupierre.

The 13th century Tour des Bouchers or Butchers' Tower separates the upper town from the lower town. It was renovated and made higher in the 16th century.

RIQUEWIHR

Riquewihr is a small town situated in the very heart of the Alsatian wine-growing area. The village was mentioned for the first time in documents dated 1049 under the name "Richovilare". In the 11th century it was part of the property of the Counts of Eguisheim before passing in the 12th century into the hands of the Counts of Horbourg who fortified it in 1291 and conferred the status of town on it in 1320. In 1324 the town was sold to the Counts of Wurtemberg while in 1397 it was joined to the county of Montbéliard following the marriage of Henriette de Montfaucon with Eberhard de Wurtemberg. The Counts of Wurtemberg retained the lordship of the estate until the Revolution. At the end of the 15th century a Council, under the supervision of the Bailiff, the count's representative, governed the town. In 1534 the Reformation was introduced in Riquewihr on the initiative of Count Georges of Wurtemberg Montbéliard.

Thanks to the vineyards and the wine trade Riquewihr enjoyed a period of great prosperity. In 1520 the Guild of Wine-growers was created whose offices today are at no. 42 Rue du Général de Gaulle. It was also in this period, about 1500, that the construction of a second city wall surrounded by a wide moat was undertaken. Certain features dating from the 13th century were incorporated into the new fortifications and altered appropriately, for example, the Thieves' Tower which owes its name to its function as a prison, and the Dolder. This high tower, which also served as a belfry, lost its role as the gateway to the town when the Porte Supérieure, furnished with a portcullis and a drawbridge, was constructed. The town's lower gateway was demolished in the 19th century. The town is laid out on either side of the main street within a quadrilateral. Of the medieval churches there remains almost nothing. The 12th century parish church was abandoned after numerous rebuildings. The church of Our Lady built in the Gothic style, was transformed into a Protestant presbytery at the time of the Reformation. St. Ehrard's church was similarly

turned into a house after being completely rebuilt.

The original castle was also demolished in order to replace it with a residence more to the taste of the period. Count George of Wurtemberg and his wife liked staying there and it even became his wife's principal residence after his death. It was finished in 1540 and was surrounded with auxiliary buildings, a chancellery, stables, etc. After the Revolution it was turned into a school.

The magnificently sumptuous houses which line the streets and alleys date from the same period. It is impossible to mention them all since almost all the dwellings in Riquewihr go back to the 16th or 17th centuries and some are even older dating from the 15th century. Two houses are absolutely typical: the house known as Jung-Selig, no. 12-14 Rue du Général de Gaulle, and the house known as Dissler at 6 Rue de la

◀ *Riquewihr: the Porte Supérieure.*

◀ *Riquewihr: the Dolder.*

Riquewihr: a typical house with cooper's tools.

Riquewihr: a house in Rue de la Couronne.

Couronne. Jung-Selig which dates from 1561 is noteworthy for its high and wide half-timbered façade. Dissler, built in 1610 by Peter Burger a member of the Town Council, illustrates the taste and wealth of the bourgeoisie of this period. This house has recently been the object of restoration by the Caisse Nationale des Monuments Historiques.

However the Thirty Years' War stopped development in this small town. In 1635 Riquewihr was besieged and then pillaged by the troops of the Duke of Lorraine. After the Treaty of Westphalia in 1648 the town remained under the lordship of the Count of Wurtemberg Montbéliard even though it was under the sovereignty of the King of France. This situation persisted up until the Revolution. Indeed it was not until 1796 that Riquewihr became a French town.

The town underwent some modification during the 19th century, the churches and the Town Hall being rebuilt. The reputation of this little town continues to grow thanks to the quality and renown of its wines but also thanks to the picturesque nature of its old streets and dwellings which make it one of the most frequently visited tourist centres in Alsace.

Riquewihr, the Rue du Général de Gaulle: ▶
Jung-Selig House and Irion House
(in the background).

Riquewihr, Kiener House: the Well (1576).

Riquewihr: Jung-Selig House,
12-14 Rue du Général de Gaulle.

Riquewihr: Preiss-Zimmer House.

THE ALSATIAN VINEYARDS

The foothills of the Vosges halfway between the plain and the high barrier of the Vosges themselves, constitute a well defined region between two hundred and four hundred metres above sea level. The climate is relatively dry and sunny and the importance which wine-growing has attained here over the last two thousand years justifies the name of Route du Vin which is given to the greater part of this line of hills. Especially from Thann and Guebwiller to Obernai, the holdings, overlooked by the silhouettes of numerous ruined castles half hidden by the nearby forest, vary as much as the soils which are the outcome of a long and complex geological history.

The villages and towns, often fortified, which line the route are evidence of the wealth provided by wine-growing and wine-making.

One has to leave Colmar, the traditional capital of the vineyards, and follow the Route du Vin from village to village to fully comprehend the way in which production is rooted in the individual holdings. The multiplicity of the terrains is one of the justifications for the planting of different types of grapes in the vineyards of this zone of "Appellation d'origine contrôlée". Riesling, the best known of all, Tokay, Gewürztraminer, Muscat, red and white Pinots and Sylvaner are the most important of these very characteristic vines. Their individual qualities make it possible to use these wines, and these alone,

Landmarks of the vineyards country producing the best Alsatian wines.

as the accompaniment to a fine meal from the aperitif to the dessert.

Techniques have evolved and the old winepresses and huge wooden barrels have given way in many cases to modern installations. However if the Alsatian wine-growers have constantly improved their methods it has been in order to advance the art of wine-making. More than ever a walk across these meticulously maintained hills and a visit to their cellars provide ample proof of the love and care with which these great wines are produced.

KAYSERSBERG

Kaysersberg, situated at the point where the valley of the river Weiss emerges into the Plain of Alsace, has a longer history than that of the castle which overlooks its vineyards and its medieval buildings. "Caesaris Mons", "The Emperor's Hill", is mentioned in the Roman period. The village and the castle were acquired by the Emperor in the 12th century and fortified, becoming a free and imperial town which in the 14th century joined the Decapole.

The castle, which was built by Frederick II of Hohenstaufen, occupies a strategic position on the road from Lorraine, passing over the Col du Bonhomme. It still has its 12th century keep with a commanding view over the houses of the town inside the wall and over the Weiss valley. At the west entrance to the town a 15th century fortified bridge with a chapel in the middle crosses the river. The houses, some of them very beautiful, give this little town a very picturesque character.

The parish church was constructed over a period lasting from the 12th to the 16th centuries. The sculpted tympanum over the doorway dates from about 1230-1235 and is a fine example of Alsatian Romanesque art. It represents the Coronation of the Virgin, flanked by the archangels Michael and Gabriel. As the inscription in the left-hand corner indicates, the small figure is Cunradus, the master mason or sculptor of the doorway. The church furniture is very rich, but particular attention should be paid to the altar-piece in the choir by Hans Bongart of Colmar which is dated 1518. The Crucifixion in the centre is surrounded by

wooden bas-reliefs representing scenes from the Passion. At the top of each panel in the fixed part there is some very delicately carved foliage.

The scenes on the moveable parts of the altarpiece are either interiors or scenes in a landscape. The predella shows Christ and the Apostles. On the top to the centre part are three painted and gilded statues: St.

Helen who found the True Cross, St. Christopher carrying the Infant Jesus on his shoulders, and St. Margaret.

Finally Kaysersberg is the birth place of an Alsatian who has become famous throughout the world — Dr. Albert Schweitzer, founder of the hospital at Lambaréné in the Republic of Gabon. Nobel Peace Prize winner in 1954, musician,

Kaysersberg: the parish church's façade.

Kaysersberg: altar-piece ▶ by Hans Bongart in the church.

philosopher and Protestant Pastor, he was born in Kaysersberg on the 14th January 1875 and died in Lambaréné in 1965.

Turckheim: the Porte de France.

Turckheim: the Town Hall and the night-watchman.

TURCKHEIM

Turckheim, a small wine-producing town near Colmar on the left bank of the river Fecht at the foot of the Brand hills, still has its city walls with three gates, the 14th century Porte de France, the Porte du Brand and the Porte de Munster. The name of Turenne remains associated with a battle won by that great strategist in 1675 in front of the city walls.

There are numerous old buildings still around which give certain spots the atmosphere of a theatrical set. For example, in the Place Turenne there is the Magistrate's house with its mullion windows, which was later turned into a guard house, there is the 16th century Town Hall with its beautiful gable and finally there is the Hôtel des Deux Clefs, with its half-timbering and its magnificent carved oriel (previously an ancient city hostelry it was renovated in 1620).

The rebuilding of St. Anne's church in the 19th century spared the belfry and porch, the lower parts of which are Romanesque and date from the 12th century while the upper parts are in the Gothic style with a steep tiled roof.

One tradition has remained very much alive in Turckheim, that of the night-watchman. During the summer he walks around the town in his loose-fitting greatcoat with his lantern and his halberd, crying out at every corner "Veillez au feu et à la lumière" (watch your fire and your lamps).

Turckheim: Hôtel des deux Clefs. ▶

Place de l'Ancienne Douane: the Koïfhus.

COLMAR

Although archeological research has furnished abundant evidence for Man's presence in the region since the Neolithic period, and the Bronze and Iron Ages have left behind some exceptional remains, Colmar does not make its appearance until much later. The important remains of the Gallo-Roman civilisation provide abundant evidence of the occupation of the countryside and of the site of Horbourg. In the 9th century Colmar, known at that time as "Columbaria", was just a vast estate, a residence used on several occasions by the Carolingian Kings.

It is between the 10th century and the beginning of the 13th century that one can situate the first important period of growth of what up to then was only a large village. Colmar was raised to the status of a municipality, then came under the direct rule of the Emperor. This political development was accompanied by the first mention of the townsfolk, the new fortifications and the presence of the Imperial Eagle on the town's seal. In 1278 Rodolph of Hapsburg granted the town a municipal constitution, the areas of competence of the provost and the council were fixed, and the townsfolk came directly under the protection of the Empire. At the end of the Middle Ages the bourgeoisie confirmed its new power through its struggle within the Decapole, that well known association of the ten Imperial towns of Alsace, against ecclesiastical and aristocratic power. Colmar at this time also became a great artistic centre.

Many workshops were set up which are reputed to have developed easel painting as well as to have produced famous panel paintings of the "late Gothic" period.

Like Renaissance Art the Protestant Reformation was late in coming to Colmar. After many vicissitudes the final outcome of the Thirty Years War saw the integration of Colmar into the possessions of the French monarchy. The arrival in 1698 of the Jesuits of Ensisheim, who installed themselves in St. Peter's Priory, demonstrated the royal wish to give the Catholic Church an important role. It was in the same year that the Sovereign Council of Alsace established itself in Colmar. It was composed of eminent jurists in whose company Voltaire, who was in Colmar during 1753-54, found consolation for his

misfortunes.

After the French revolution Colmar became integrated even further into the French administration. Naturally the urban development during the period of German annexation from 1870 to 1918 changed the appearance of some streets and squares but it must be stated that the contemporary development of Colmar has occurred without any sudden break with its past. The changes during the 19th century together with the ravages of two world wars fortunately have not deprived Colmar of its past and the town has retained this heritage while witnessing an unprecedented growth since 1945.

KOÏFHUS

This complex of buildings was the very heart of the economic and political life of Colmar during the Middle Ages. The first floor of the main building of the Koïfhus or old Customs House was occupied by the town administration while the ground floor was a goods warehouse. It was surrounded by other buildings now long gone, the Grande Boucherie (the Abattoir or Slaughterhouse), the Eisenhaus or depository for iron and other metals, the Ankenhaus for fats, the monetary workshop, the Corn Exchange and the Salt Exchange.

The oldest building in the Koïfhus complex, built in yellow sandstone from Rouffach, was finished in 1480. It is a vast two-storied rectangular building with a steeply pitched roof and a large doorway together with a smaller side door.

One finds the same arrangement of doors on the north side, which allows vehicles loaded with merchandise to cross the hall to unload it. The windows are characteristically Gothic — rectangular with moulded mullions. The interior is very sobre, wooden ceilings being supported by stone pillars. On the first floor the stained glass windows depict the coats of arms of the towns belonging to the Decapole whose representatives met here.

To this, the main and the oldest part of the complex, is joined a

The Koïfhus: eastern façade.

*Place de l'Ancienne Douane:
the Schwendi fountain.*

Rue des Marchands.

Pfister House. ▶

smaller building. This has an arcaded ground floor with above it a loggia giving on to the Place de l'Ancienne Douane. On the west side, access to the rooms is via a double flight of stairs with stone banisters.

The complex is completed by a third building constructed at the end of the 16th century as a market for butter and imported fats.

In 1897 a stone fountain was erected having an eight-sided basin and a tall central pillar on which is a bronze statue by Auguste Bartholdi of Baron Lazare of Schwendi, the lord of Holandsberg (1522-1583).

THE RUE DES MARCHANDS

It was only in 1783 that Schädelgasse, Skull Street, changed its name to Rue des Marchands. There are numerous houses in this street which have the characteristic architecture of 16th century Colmar. The ground floors are stone with moulded doorways, sometimes arched, while the upper floors are half-timbered, often overhanging. The great age of these houses is attested to by the dates which are engraved on the lintels of the doors or on the keystones of the arches. Some are still decorated with old painted signs.

The house at no. 52 takes its name, "The Bear", from the sculpted figure of a bear which used to be on the corner. The house at no. 42 is interesting because it is still laid out in the form of a 16th century artisan's atelier or workshop.

On the same side no. 34, "Zum grienen Hus", the Green House, was that of the Colmar painter Gaspard Isenmann.

The house at no. 30, now the Bartholdi Museum, is the birth place of the Colmar sculptor Auguste Bartholdi. It is an 18th century town house, largely rebuilt in the 19th century but still retaining many elements of its original style.

Pfister house was built in 1537 by the toque merchant Ludwig Scherer on the site of an older house. By 1567 it belonged to a draper, Claus Stattmann, to whom we are indebted for the external mural decoration. In 1596 it belonged to yet another merchant who had it restored in 1613. The name it now bears is that of the 19th century proprietors.

The house was restored in 1971. It is a vast three story house in Rouffach limestone with a very fine oriel window on the corner. The mullion windows are still in the Gothic tradition. The wooden gallery on the second floor is supported by stone consoles. The upper floors are reached by a spiral staircase in the octagonal turret. However this building is particularly noteworthy for its mural decoration.

The iconography is characteristic

of humanist taste of the period associating as it does Biblical themes (the four Evangelists, the Fathers of the Church, in the bottom row; scenes from Genesis in the second row; and other scenes from the Old Testament in the third row) with allegorical figures (Love, Faith, Justice, Hope, Force and Temperance in the third row) and effigies of Emperors (Maximilian, Charles, Ferdinand) under the second floor gallery.

PLACE DE LA CATHÉDRALE

The square was created in 1784 on the site of the former St. Martin's cemetery. There are two buildings worthy of note. Firstly, Adolph House, named after the 19th century owner who uncovered the Gothic windows. The oldest parts of the house date from the 14th century, but the building underwent alterations in the 16th century particularly to the ground floor as is shown by the date, 1584, on the side door. The upper part with its half-timbering is similarly a later addition.

The old guard house was constructed in 1575 on the site of St. James' Chapel which had been the chapel of St. Martin's cemetery since the 13th century. The decoration, which is of very fine quality, is concentrated on the semicircular main entrance and on the loggia. The richness in the ornamentation is shown by decorative motifs such as the muzzles of lions, masks, and iron-work motifs arranged as a frieze on the loggia. This building is considered to be among the most beautiful remaining from the second half of the 16th century in Alsace.

THE COLLEGIATE CHURCH OF ST. MARTIN

St. Martin's church in Colmar is one of the most beautiful examples of Gothic architecture still extant in the Haut-Rhin. Its great size is undoubtedly the reason it is often wrongly described as a "cathedral".

Recent excavations, however, have revealed that from the 11th century there existed a church with a square choir and a projecting transept. It was only in 1235 that St. Martin's became a collegiate church and was reconstructed.

The work on the new church, which was in the Gothic style, started on the eastern side with the construction of the transept between 1240 and 1260 or thereabouts. The

Place de la Cathédrale: Adolph's House.

Old Guard House.

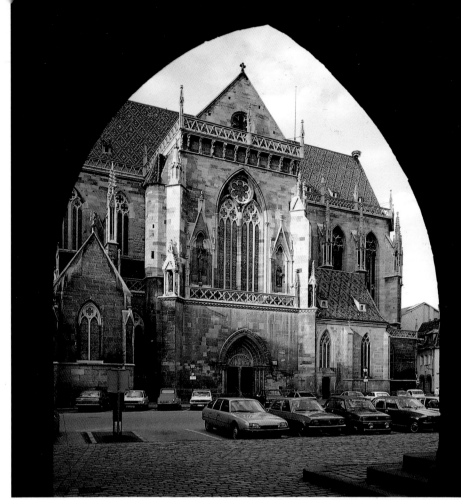

*The Collegiate church
of St. Martin: south façade.*

*The Collegiate church
of St. Martin: interior.*

The Dominican church.

tympanum above the doorway in the south façade shows, arranged concentrically, a Last Judgement above the legend of St. Nicholas. The nave which was finished about 1270, testifies, by its refusal to imitate Strasbourg Cathedral which must have been the model at the time, to the great variety of Gothic forms existing in Alsace. The west face was intended to have a harmonious façade with two towers but only the south tower was ever finished. It was finished in the middle of the 14th century.

The second important phase of the Gothic rebuilding was the reconstruction of the Choir. This was probably conceived by Master William of Marburg before 1350 and was carried out before 1360. The plan of the choir is somewhat unusual. It is surrounded by a series of intercommunicating chapels which are situated between the buttresses. Together with the doorways, the sculpted consoles illustrating the Passion of Christ which decorate the upper parts of the walls, constitute the major part of the older decoration of the building.

The stained-glass windows date mainly from the beginning of the 20th century with the exception of three beautiful scenes from the Old Testament and the Passion in the north bay of the narthex of St. Martin's.

THE CHURCH OF THE DOMINICANS

During the 13th and 14th centuries Colmar saw the foundation of the churches of the Dominicans, of the Dominican Nuns of Unterlinden and of St. Catherine, and of the Franciscans.

The Dominican ideals of poverty and austerity are reflected in the structure of their church. The very long ambulatory is supported by simple buttresses and the bell tower is reduced to its simplest possible form. The most astonishing feature is the way the space inside the church is exploited. The use of tall columns into which the great arcades penetrate directly without the use of intervening capitals breaks up the space very little giving an impression of unity which is reinforced by the very small difference in height between the central nave and the side aisles which have wooden ceilings. The choir on the other hand is vaulted with pointed arches.

Martin Schongauer's
Virgin of the Rose Bush.

The Virgin of the Rose Bush, Martin Schongauer's masterpiece painted in 1473 for the Collegiate Church of St. Martin is on temporary exhibition in the church.

Martin Schongauer, who was almost certainly born in Colmar round about 1450 and whose father came from Augsburg, shows the Virgin and Child seated on a lawn with rose bushes in the background on which birds are perched.

Two angels hovering above hold the Virgin's crown. Here Schongauer is taking up the theme of the Virgin in the garden but he manages to combine a monumental force with the tenderness of the subject to create one of the great masterpieces of North European painting in the late Middle Ages.

◄The Maison des Têtes.

Unterlinden Museum
(former Dominican convent).

THE MAISON DES TÊTES

It was this house, constructed in 1609 for the Colmar merchant Anton Burger, which gave its name in 1888 to the street in which it stands. The style of the façade, the mullion windows, the tall fluted gable, are all features very similar to those of other buildings of the same period in Colmar, for example, the Maison Kern and the Place du Marché-aux-fruits. However what distinguishes this building is the profusion of decorative elements — caryatides, heads, and grimacing masks — which moreover are not simply limited to the frames of the doorway and the oriel but are also to be found on the jambs and mullions of the windows. It does not appear, however, that the overall scheme is the result of any coherent iconographic plan. On top of the gable there is a statue representing an Alsatian cooper. It dates from 1902 and is the work of Auguste Bartholdi.

THE CONVENT OF THE DOMINICAN NUNS OF UNTERLINDEN

The Museum is in the former convent of the Dominican Nuns of Unterlinden which was founded at the beginning of the 13th century by two aristocratic widows from Colmar, Agnès de Mittelnheim and Agnès de Hergheim. In 1252 the nuns established themselves for good in the place known as Sub Tillia (underneath the lime trees or Unter den Linden). The convent soon assumed considerable importance both material and spiritual. In 1269 the choir of the church was consecrated by Albert the Great, Bishop of Ratisbonne. In 1289 the cloisters were finished. The wealth and fame of the Unterlinden nuns continued to increase up until the 15th century. The 16th century however saw the beginning of the decline of the convent. In the 18th century the convent must have taken on a new lease of life, since there are alterations to the buildings dating from this period. An extra storey was added to the cloisters and the nave of the chapel was modified. In 1792 the sisters finally left the convent.

The building was saved from demolition in 1849 by Louis Hugot who two years before had created

*Unterlinden Museum,
wine-grower's cellar: old presses.*

Unterlinden Museum: the Chapel. ▶

the Société Schongauer. In fact by installing the Roman mosaic from Bergheim in the former convent and by moving a collection of old paintings there in 1852 the Société Schongauer laid the basis for the Museum.

The Medieval architecture of the Dominican Convent of Unterlinden makes it a site of exceptional quality for the museum's collections which have not stopped growing since 1849. Although the most famous of its works, such as the panel paintings of Martin Schongauer and the Colmar School, the Issenheim altar-piece by Grünewald and the Romanesque and Gothic sculptures, blend in particularly well with this medieval building it should not be forgotten that the Unterlinden Museum also attempts to put on display a much wider view of the history of art and of civilisation.

The Archeological Section allows us to follow technical development from the polished stone tools of the Neolithic Period to the jewelry of the Bronze and Iron Ages. The Gallo-Roman Period is richly documented on living conditions and all aspects of daily life, thanks to the floor mosaic from Bergheim, and on religious beliefs and practices, thanks to funerary stones and the statues of Roman and Gaulish divinities.

The quality of Merovingian bronze fibulae blends smoothly into that of the following period. However the Middle Ages is represented mainly by a series of Romanesque sculptures including several consoles from the former church at Alspach. The Gothic Period is well represented by sculptures from the 13th, 14th and particularly the 15th centuries, by a large number of painted panels, from the anony-

mous painters of the beginning of the 15th century to Gaspard Isenmann and Schongauer, as well as by the minor arts among which should be noted a very rare Alsatian tapestry on the theme of the Fountain of Youth.

For the Modern Period from the Renaissance to the beginning of the 20th century precise military and historical mementos can be contrasted with the popular arts and traditions. These illustrate the way in which local customs are rooted in such things as painted furniture, costume, household utensils, the tools of the wine-maker, the wine-press and the wine-cellar with its decorated barrels. It is more than 20 years now since the Musée d'Unterlinden opened its doors to contemporary art.

The majestic ensemble, usually simply called "the Issenheim altarpiece", with its associated sculp-

tures and paintings, constituted the main altar of that monastery. It consists on the one hand of a series of wooden sculptures executed at the end of the 15th century by the artist Nicolas de Haguenau and on the other hand of a series of painted panels, either fixed or pivoting like shutters in front of the sculptures, the work of an exceptional master who has been much studied and yet of whom we still know little, to whom the name of Grünewald is most correctly given. These paintings were executed probably between 1512 and 1516.

The precious and exceptional nature of this artistic ensemble does not allow this transformable altar-piece to be exhibited as originally intended. The Unterlinden Museum, in whose possession it is, has found it necessary to exhibit the different panels separately in order to avoid constant handling, which would be extremely deleterious to its good conservation. After seeing the tragic interpretation of the Cruci-fixion, which is flanked by the monumental figures of St. Sebastian

Grünewald's Issenheim altar-piece: the Angel's Concert and the Nativity.

on the left and of St. Anthony on the right, and which is placed above a predella showing the Entombment, the visitor is forced to use his imagination in order to reconstitute

the sight which the opening of the first set of shutters would have revealed. This would have consisted of Grünewald's rendering of, in sequence, the Annunciation, the concert of Angels, the Nativity and the Resurrection which are now exhibited separately. The opening of the second set of shutters revealed to view the other two painted panels, the Temptation of St. Anthony and the Visit of St. Anthony to St. Paul, which flanked the central group of sculptures: St. Augustin, St. Anthony and St.Jerome above the Christ and the Apostles of the predella. This ensemble remains one of the great masterpieces of the entire history of painting.

THE TANNERS' DISTRICT

This district is another reminder of a particular economic activity since up until the 18th century it was, in fact, entirely reserved for tanners. It has been restored thanks to the efforts of the Caisse Nationale des Monuments Historiques and of the Town of Colmar. The houses, sited for the most part along the waterway, are absolutely typical. Very narrow and very tall, and built without basements, they rest on a high stone wall the upper stories having half-timbered cob-walls made from a mixture of straw and clay. The roofs are very extensive often having openings at several different levels, some set back relative to the others, thus permitting the tanners to dry their skins.

For the most part the houses date from the 16th, 17th and 18th centuries but the district itself is very much older. In fact the Rue des Tanneurs was enlarged in the 14th century and then again in 1883. Up until the French Revolution beside the waterway, the mill canal or "tanners ditch" as it was called, there used to stand a tower, the Tanners' or Witches' Tower, against which stood St. Michael's Chapel, mentioned in the 12th century, and a part of the original town wall.

The Rue du Chasseur.

La Grand'Rue.

The Rue Saint-Jean.

The Place des ▶
Six Montagnes Noires.

Little Venice. ▶

THE PLACE DES SIX MONTAGNES NOIRES

This square owes its name to a hostelry, the most important in the Middle Ages, which stood on the site until 1880. The Roesselmann fountain, the work of Bartholdi, was installed there in 1882. In 1265 Jean Roesselmann, the town Provost, succeeded in retaking Colmar from the nobles and the supporters of the Bishop of Strasbourg, by whom he had been expelled, after re-entering it hidden in a barrel.

From the Place des Six Montagnes Noires two parallel streets lead to the Koïfhus. The Grand' Rue, is lined on both sides by a lot of fine houses of which many are timbered, no. 84 being particularly picturesque with its two overhanging upper floors. The Rue Saint-Jean owes its name to the Order of St. John whose knights settled in Colmar during the first half of the 13th century. Of the church consecrated by Albert the Great in 1268 there remains only the choir, extensively rebuilt in the 19th century, and a trefoiled doorway supported by short columns and decorated on the corner stones with leaf heads. Another important building in this street is the one called the House of the Knights of St. John which was constructed in 1608 for a Colmar family by the architect Albrecht Schmidt.

LITTLE VENICE

The Krutenau is a district inhabited by market-gardeners to the west of the Lauch river. Its main street is the Rue Turenne. This area is also called Little Venice because of the waterway lined with picturesque houses which runs through it. Although it has existed since 1209 it was originally outside the fortifications of the town and was only incorporated into it in 1250. The bridge across the Lauch was formerly the entrance to the town itself. It was also called "the bridge by the watering place" because of the large area on its right where the market-gardeners watered their animals in the river.

EGUISHEIM

The wine-growing market town of Eguisheim owes its reputation to the exceptional quality of its rows of old houses which are remarkably well preserved, as well as to the wines produced by the vineyards which surround it. One can walk round this small town by following the old ramparts which like the houses are built around the castle in the centre, the residence of the bishop's bailiff, the 13th century remains of the castle are now completely lost in the midst of all the 19th century reconstructions.

The village was formerly the property of the d'Eguisheim family, one member of which, Bruno, Count d'Eguisheim, became Pope Leo IX in 1048. When the family became extinct it was acquired by the Bishop of Strasbourg who had the walls built. The church of St. Peter and St. Paul is apt to be over-

Eguisheim: typical houses.

Eguisheim: the interior of the church.

looked. Despite its modern reconstruction it has retained a Gothic bell-tower and above all an important example of Alsatian Romanesque sculpture — the doorway, executed in the first half of the 13th century. The tympanum shows Christ with his right hand raised in blessing, flanked by the apostles Peter and Paul. On the left lintel the five Wise Virgins with their lamps advance towards the open door where Christ is waiting for them. On the right lintel the five Foolish Virgins stand in front of the closed door with their upturned lamps in their hands.

The silhouettes of the three castles of Eguisheim overlook the village and vineyard of Husseren from the first forest-covered slopes of the hill. The castle of Haut-Eguisheim is the oldest fort in Alsace according to the documentary evidence, since it is mentioned as early as the 11th century. The surviving building, together with those of the neighbouring Pflixbourg and Haut-Landsberg castles, dates essentially from the 12th and 13th centuries.

ROUFFACH

Much more than the old houses which line its narrow streets, it is the area around the very beautiful and unfinished old church of Our Lady (it must have seen a succession of master-masons and sculptors working on it between the 12th and 15th centuries) which expresses the special something which is Rouffach. The Place de la République, lined with large public buildings, reflects the opulence and importance Rouffach had in the past. In the background can be seen the medieval Witch's Tower but the most beautiful buildings, both for their architecture and for their dimensions, are arranged around this big square. There is the Corn Exchange dating from 1524, the Town Hall with its double staircase and its saw-tooth gable, and the office of the tax collector of the Cathedral Chapter of Strasbourg (of which Rouffach was a dependency) with a double gable and balustrades bearing the arms of Rohan.

Husseren village with the three Castles of Eguisheim.

Rouffach: an ancient house in Rue Poincaré.

MUNSTER

Munster, situated right in the foot-hills of the Vosges at the point where the two valleys of the Fecht meet, owes more to the fame of its cheese than to the picturesque appearance of its streets. Although of ancient origin it was severely damaged during the first world war and was completely rebuilt in 1918. It is now a resort town and the starting point for magnificent walks in the nearby Vosges mountains.

THE BALLON D'ALSACE

The Grand Ballon, the high point of the Vosges at an altitude of 1424 metres, and the Ballon d'Alsace, 1250 metres high, with their heavily wooded slopes and their bare summits, are so called at least as much in honour of the Celtic god Belen as because of their rounded shape. The peaks of the High Vosges do have this appearance, covered in stubble and arid moors which serve as pasture for the cows whose milk goes to make Munster cheese. The Route des Crêtes or Peak Path, which has become very touristy, is

Munster: view of the city.

Murbach: the Abbey.

punctuated with "marcairies", summer farms which for the most part have been converted into farm-hotels. The numerous small lakes, hollowed out by the glaciers into natural arenas and surrounded by thick fir woods, are another great attraction of this part of the Vosges.

MURBACH

Almost lost in the bottom of a small valley at the foot of the Grand Ballon, and surrounded by forest, Murbach is a very old town dating back to the 8th century. Its abbey acquired considerable auton-

omy from episcopal authority. The bishop recognised its right to own its estate and to choose its own order, its abbot and the saint to whom its church should be dedicated. The new church was called St. Leger and placed itself under the Benedictine order.

Murbach became one of the great abbeys of Alsace and the equal of the great religious centres of the Rhine valley. The monastery grew in political power and in spiritual influence.

Abbot Bertolf (1122-1149) was almost certainly behind the decision to rebuild the church, of which only the eastern parts remain, the

choir with a flat ambulatory flanked on each side with chapels on two levels, and the protruding transept with its two towers. The harmony and equilibrium of the building are exceptional as is the very high quality of the sculpted decoration.

The abbey started to decline in the 14th century. In the middle of the 17th century the church and the monastery buildings were sacked by the troops of the Duke of Weimar. After Alsace became part of France there was a timid attempt to reconstruct the abbey but it was finally dismantled and its goods dispersed during the French Revolution.

GUEBWILLER

Guebwiller, one of the more southerly of the small towns along the Route du Vin in Alsace, is a spot which has many things in its favour. The town is situated on the right bank of the river Lauch near the spot where the Lauch valley runs into the Plain of Alsace. The name "Florival" which is given to this valley in itself suggests the nature of the landscape one finds there. One should not fail to visit the Romanesque churches at Murbach and Lautenbach in the Lauch valley.

Guebwiller has taken advantage of its situation and has based its development on various resources: the vineyards, of course, but industry also plays a very important role. From its Medieval past there remain several essential features. St. Léger church, constructed at the end of the 12th and the beginning of the 13th centuries, shows the persistence in Alsatian architecture of Romanesque forms even in cases where certain Gothic techniques, such as the pointed vault, are used. To each of the vaults over the square bays of the central nave there correspond two bays in the aisles, and to this alternation of the supports is added a towering interior elevation; there is a large expanse of bare wall above the huge arcades, the high windows opening only a small part of the wall. Similarly the conception of the capitals and of the doorway is similar to that of 12th century Alsatian churches. Comparison with the apse which was reconstructed in the 14th century emphasizes the differences even more.

The Dominican Monastery which was built at the beginning of the 14th century adopts many features of the architecture of the Mendicant Orders in Alsace but in an original way, as is shown in particular by its wide rood screen.

The church of Our Lady which is connected with the transfer of the

*Guebwiller: the exterior
of the Church of Our Lady.*

Guebwiller: Church of St. Léger.

Benedictine Community from the abbey at Murbach in 1759, is an important example of 18th century religious architecture. The building was started by Beuque and then continued by G.I. Ritter after 1768. It has a majestic interior elevation in which tall Corinthian columns separate the nave from the aisles. Although only the south tower was ever completed and that somewhat belatedly, the pink limestone façade deserves to occupy a position of distinction in French Classical Art.

Thann: panoramic view.

THANN

The foundation of Thann only goes back to the second half of the 12th century. At first it was only a centre of pilgrimage originating from the vision of Count Eberhardt. One evening looking out from his castle, Engelbourg, which overlooks the site, he was intrigued by a light shining in the valley and going down, he met the servant of the dead saint Thiébaut, bishop of Gubbio, who could not remove his pilgrim's staff from the trunk of a tree on which he had rested it. Count Eberhardt interpreted this as the saint's wish to see a chapel established on that spot. Since then every year on St. Thiébaut's day

three fir trees are burned to commemorate Count Eberhardt's vision.

An important centre of pilgrimage in the Middle Ages, the church was rebuilt in the middle of the 14th century. Although a fairly small church, the quality of its architecture and of its decoration make it one of the most beautiful Gothic buildings in the region.

The construction of the church continued from the 14th to the 16th centuries under the direction of various master masons. The work started in 1342 with the nave and then proceeded with the choir and the north tower which was finished at the beginning of the 15th century by Master Werlin, the

Thann, St. Thiébaut's Church: a detail of the main door.

Thann, St. Thiébaut's Church: the main door.

vaulting being in the flamboyant style. In 1456 the north aisle with its huge windows was finished. But without a doubt the greatest of the master masons was Master Rémy Faesch from Basle who between 1506 and 1516 built, among other things, the magnificent open-work spire which dominates Thann.

The stained glass in the choir dates from the middle of the 15th century and illustrates scenes from Genesis, the Ten Commandments, the Passion of Christ, the Life of the Virgin and the lives of St. Thiébaut, St. Catherine and the Alsatian saints. The choir stalls, dating from 1450, were extensively restored at the beginning of this century.

On the outside the west door (1400) is richly decorated with scenes from the life of the Virgin Mary arranged in five rows. The two small tympana, between which stands a statue of the Virgin and Child, illustrate the Crucifixion and the Nativity. On the jambs there are figures of saints and in particular a very beautiful St. George and the Dragon.

The north door, which dates from the middle of the 15th century, is treated in a more ornamental style and has two very fine statues of St. Thiébaut and St. John-the-Baptist at either side of the Virgin and Child on the central pier.

MULHOUSE

Originally just a mill on the bank of the river Ill, the old centre of Mulhouse developed between the 12th and 13th centuries. Mulhouse became a city of the Holy Roman Empire in 1293 and joined the Decapole in 1354. However because of its isolated position in the south of the province, in its struggles with the aristocracy it was towards the Swiss towns that it turned for help, first to Berne and Soleure and later to Basle, which in 1506 offered it protection. Finally in 1515 the republic of Mulhouse signed a pact allying it with the Helvetic Confederation. In spite of the treaty of Westphalia, Mulhouse remained independent until 1798 when it was joined to France. In the course of the 19th century the town was completely transformed by the growth of various industries and in particular the textile industry.

Although the picturesque side of the town has almost completely disappeared, it must be pointed out that it has become the home of several technical museums, the Musée de l'Impression sur Etoffes (the Museum of Printed Fabrics), the Musée du Chemin-de-Fer (Railway Museum), and the Musée de l'Automobile (the Car Museum).

A relic of a time now long gone, the Bollwerk, one of the 14th century city gates, in now completely surrounded by the modern town. The old centre is concentrated around the Place de la Réunion. Even the church of St. Stephen was rebuilt in neo-Gothic style by the Mulhouse architect Jean-Baptiste Schacre. True it is on the site of the 14th century church whose stained glass was saved and used.

The Town Hall, built after 1552, is noteworthy for the murals on the façade. The huge allegorical figures of Virtues are the work of Christian Bockstorffer of Constanz. The theme was taken up again in the 17th century by the Mulhouse artist Jean Gabriel. The Council Chamber has preserved its wainscoting and civic stained glass and now houses Mulhouse's Musée Historique.

Mulhouse: the Town Hall.

Mulhouse: St. Stephen's Church.

THE FRENCH RAILWAY MUSEUM
(Musée Français du Chemin de Fer)

The French Railway Museum (Musée Français du Chemin de Fer) owns the most important collection of rolling-stock material in continental Europe. The visitor can admire not just the evolution of steam, electric and diesel engines, dating from the beginning of railroads up until the Fifties, but also the truly sumptuous passenger carriages, from a mid-20th-century diligence on wheels to the magnificent luxury coaches of the Twenties and Thirties and the Presidential carriage used by General de Gaulle.

The collection also illustrates other sectors of considerable interest, such as railway lines, signals, buildings, civil works and telecommunications. The Railway Museum represents an instrument of communication, an exceptional space: a visit there becomes an enthralling adventure.

THE NATIONAL AUTOMOBILE MUSEUM
(Musée National de l'Automobile)

The Automobile Museum in Mulhouse is the most prestigious in the world, with more than 500 vehicles in the collection. One hundred and two different makes are represented in the 446 automobiles on exhibition, of which 66 are of French make. All periods of French production are present, from 1878 to the present.

The collection of Bugattis is unique, with 112 models including prototypes of which only one example was made. The Schlumpf collection can thus the visited in an area which measures 20,000 m² and with a route almost two kms long, decorated with period lamps.

This page, above: 1882 Forquenot P.O. steam engine, on display at the French Railway Museum. Centre and below: two cars in the Schlumpf Collection, at the National Automobile Museum.

The Tour de l'Europe in Mulhouse, 100
meters high.

The characteristic 14th-c. Bollwerk.

Place des Victoires in Mulhouse.

The typical Hotel Guillaume Tell.

Four views of the characteristic Ecomusée d'Alsace.

THE ECONOMUSEUM OF ALSACIA
(Ecomusée d'Alsace)

The Ecomuseum of Alsace is a walk through time which begins with the fortified 12th-century house and in the course of which the visitor traverses all the great events which have left their mark in the history of Alsace.

A walk through time, but also through space, discovering the various Alsatian territories, or a walk in the past through crafts and techniques that once were, thanks to the way in which the Ecomuseum has been installed with permanent exhibitions of houses as they are being built, thus showing us the various faces of work. The blacksmith, the cobbler, the baker, the oil-presser, the cartwright, bring back to life all those gestures which seemed forgotten. Of course, there are also the farm animals, including the storks which make their nests in the village rooftops.

This village has been created thanks to the enthusiasm of a group of volunteers and the receptiveness of the local organizations.

It is hard to imagine that in 1980 this land was nothing but a deserted heath.

The houses that have been rebuilt and presented here had all been marked for destruction. Of the hundreds of other buildings which were to be demolished, these were singled out and saved as being typical of the Alsatian territory, of a specific period or because they had a specific social function.

Thanks to the participation of public institutions as well as private institutions, the Ecomuseum therefore plays a part in safeguarding and evaluating outstanding examples of the patrimony of the region. On the one hand, in the sense that it is regional it serves to remind the inhabitants of Alsace of their past and helps them transmit this past to their children. At the same time, it allows visitors from other regions and other countries to understand Alsace, to know the traditional customs and costumes.

But the museum is not limited to rural architecture and agriculture. It has also undertaken the difficult task of restoring the Potassium mine Rodolphe and has also decided to collect objects from the amusement parks of once upon a time, committing itself to bring back to France the carousel known as «Célèbre Carrousel-Salon Demeyer», which has been abroad for almost thirty years.

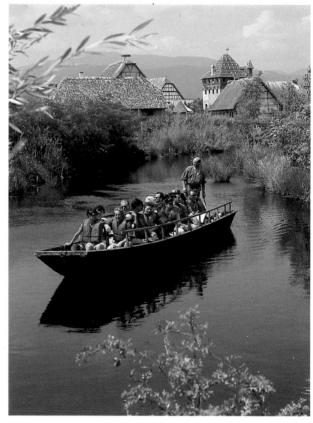

HUNAWIHR

THE LIVE EXOTIC BUTTERFLY CENTRE

We are glad to offer you a splendid collection of exotic butterflies which live, free, in a luxuriant flora: a collection of orchids and of passion flowers.

Strolling through the botanical park or through the green-houses, the visitor discovers the fascinating and defenceless life of butterflies, following their entire life cycle from their birth.

THE ALSATIAN STORK RECOVERY CENTRE

The Centre now houses about 200 storks. Its aim is to have storks return to the Alsatian villages. Since 1976, from 30 to 50 couples reproduce in our park and in most of Alsatian and German villages. They represent about 80% of the total amount of storks present in the whole region.

Projects have aimed at organizing, in the best possible way, the natural environment destined to these birds so that they can live in total freedom. Since 1981 a show with the fishing animals is held regularly every afternoon.

A large aquarium was opened in 1983. It was made to house several cold water aquariums thus enabling the visitor to see over 20 species of fish which are original of the region.

A typical exotic butterfly from the Butterfly Glass-House.

Storks and a seal at the Stork Recovery Centre.